GOLDEN AUSTRALIAN LIBRARY

Australian Wildlife

GOLDEN AUSTRALIAN LIBRARY

Australian Wildlife

Written by Sheena Coupe
Photography by Australian
Picture Library

GOLDEN PRESS
Sydney • Auckland

First published 1982
by Golden Press Pty Ltd,
2-12 Tennyson Road, Gladesville,
NSW 2111, Australia
and 16 Copsey Place, Avondale,
Auckland 7, New Zealand.

© Australian Picture Library 1982
ISBN O 85558 861 6

Produced for the publisher by
HEL Productions Pty Ltd
Designed by Robyn Peacock-Smith
Typeset by Netan Pty Ltd
Printed by Dai Nippon Printing Company, Hong Kong

Contents

Marsupials

Marsupials are undoubtedly the most typical and distinctive Australian animals. Kangaroos, wallabies, wombats, koalas, possums, bandicoots: they are all marsupials.

More than a hundred million years ago, marsupials roamed the earth. They came to Australia across a series of land bridges that once joined the continent with Asia to the north.

Then the sea level rose and the land bridges were submerged. In most other parts of the world the primitive marsupials were displaced by stronger, more developed placental mammals. But Australia was isolated, an island sanctuary for marsupials. As they spread over the continent, safe from predators, the marsupials thrived.

These ancestral marsupials displayed an amazing ability to adapt to their environment. Today there are at least 120 marsupial species in Australia, ranging from the mighty red kangaroo to the tiny marsupial mice and planigales. Some marsupials are carnivores, others eat only plants; some live in trees, others dig burrows in the ground; some glide, others hop; some dwell in dense rainforests, others thrive in the arid plains.

But all these species have one thing in common. Unlike other mammals, a female marsupial does not have a well-developed placenta. She cannot support her foetus for very long in the womb. All marsupial babies, therefore, are born while they are still underdeveloped. These tiny, premature, half-formed creatures struggle through their mother's fur to a pouch, or *marsupium,* where they live, suckle and grow until they are sufficiently mature to survive alone.

Koalas and Wombats

With its thick woolly fur, ungainly bulky shape, leathery nose and button-like eyes, the koala is the most appealing of the marsupials. Yet this distinctive symbol of Australia is only now recovering from a protracted and ferocious attack by white settlers. Until late in the 1920s these harmless, slow-moving creatures were mercilessly hunted for their fur. In one year alone, 1924, about two million koala skins were exported, some disguised as wombat skins to spare the sensitivities of their recipients.

Koalas are tree-dwellers and they rarely move from the tree tops unless they are crossing to another home. During the day they snooze curled in a fork or straddling a limb, their strong claws keeping them firmly in place. At night they awaken to forage for food. Koalas are extra-ordinarily fussy eaters, accepting the leaves of only about a dozen species of eucalypts. An adult will eat more than a kilogram of these leaves at a sitting. They supply both nourishment and fluid, for the koala drinks almost no water.

Koalas are slow breeders and a female will usually produce one baby every two years. The tiny, blind koala, which may be only two centimetres long and weigh just five grams, struggles through its mother's fur to her pouch where it suckles for six months. Then the mother carries it on her back for a further six months until it is old enough to fend for itself.

9

Above: A family of wombats. Although they live in burrows under the ground rather than in the tree tops, wombats probably shared the same ancestors as koalas. They use their front claws as bulldozers to dig out soil for a tunnel up to 20 metres long and a metre wide.

Right: A quokka, or short-tailed pademelon, from Rottnest Island off the West Australian coast.

Kangaroos and Wallabies

Australia boasts 45 species of kangaroos, wallaroos, euros, wallabies, potoroos and rat-kangaroos, all marsupials of the macropod, or 'great foot' family. Although they vary enormously in size and habitat, all the macropods share many common characteristics. They have large hind limbs to make hopping easier and heavy tails that act as balances when they are leaping. Over millions of years their teeth and digestive systems have become adapted for grazing.

Despite these similarities, the many species of macropods have evolved in distinctive ways. The largest species, the red kangaroo, grows 160 centimetres tall and inhabits the central plains. The grey or forester kangaroo, which is almost as large, prefers the coastal scrub. Much smaller are the swamp-dwelling quokkas and the brush-tailed rock wallabies which live near rocky outcrops and boulders. In the northernmost parts of Australia two species of tree-dwelling kangaroo still exist.

Left: The red or plains kangaroo is the largest macropod. It can travel up to 50 kilometres an hour and leap nine metres in a single bound. The female is smaller than the male shown here and because of her smoky blue colour, is sometimes called a 'blue flyer'.

Above: A rare albino wallaby and joey.

11

Kangaroos and wallabies vary enormously in their size and preferred habitat. The bottom picture shows a joey developing in its mother's pouch. Baby kangaroos spend only about 33 days in the womb but for the next 190 days suckle and grow in the safety of the pouch.

Possums and Gliders

Like other marsupials possums, or phalangers as they are more accurately called, come in all shapes and sizes. Largest of all, and weighing almost seven kilograms, is the cuscus, a strange beady-eyed creature that looks rather like a particularly furry monkey. Then there are the well-known possums, the brushtails and ringtails, that are common throughout much of Australia.

Most amazing of all are the gliders, possum species that can launch themselves from high in a tree and glide gracefully to a lower branch. The brushtails, ringtails and pigmies have all evolved a gliding species. From the brushtails comes the common sugar glider; from the ringtails, the large greater glider; and from the pigmies, the tiny feathertail glider. Gliders have a flap or web of skin between their limbs. As they stretch their limbs this membrane becomes taut and the tail acts as a rudder while the glider parachutes itself through the air.

Five Australian phalangers.

Far left: A spotted cuscus from northern Queensland.

Above left: A brushtail possum.

Above top: Leadbeater's possum, a rare species from Victoria.

Left: A ringtail possum, named because of its curled tail.

Above: A sugar glider about to launch itself from a tree.

Marsupial Meateaters

Millions of years ago giant marsupial lions and tigers roamed Australia. They, of course, have long since disappeared but their descendants — marsupial carnivores, or meateaters — remain.

The largest marsupial carnivores, like the tiger cat and Tasmanian devil, stalk and eat birds, reptiles, wallabies — in fact, anything they can kill. But most of the meateaters are much smaller than these fierce species and eat only insects. Smallest of all are the marsupial mice and phascogales, tiny rat-like creatures with alert, sharp faces and equally sharp teeth. Unique among the carnivores is the striped numbat, a marsupial anteater whose diet consists almost entirely of termites — it eats up to 10 000 a day.

Like other marsupials, the carnivores give birth to tiny, unformed young that are protected by the mother until they have developed. But many carnivores have a shallow depression instead of the deep pouches of kangaroos, wallabies and koalas.

Five of the 38 species of Australian marsupial meateaters: native cat or tiger cat (top left); marsupial mole (far left); Tasmanian devil (centre left); hairy-footed dunnart (above); numbat (left). The carnivores are the most ancient of the continent's marsupials.

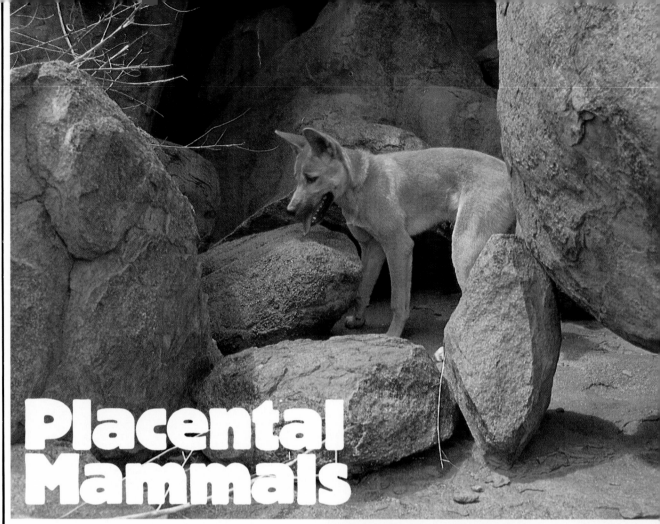

Placental Mammals

Australian marsupials are justly famous the world over. Their distinctive appearance, however, has obscured another group of Australian animals, the placental mammals whose young develop within the womb, nourished by the placenta until they are well formed.

In size the placental mammals range from the thick-set sea lion, almost four metres high, to the tiny native mice and bush rats, no bigger than their introduced rodent relatives. In habitat, too, these placental mammals vary. While seals live in the freezing waters of southern Australia, hopping mice thrive in the semi-arid deserts of the interior of the continent. There are water rats that have developed webbed feet to help them live in swamps and marshes, and tree rats in the north and northwest that spend their lives in trees and build nests in hollow branches.

Among the most common placental mammals are the 50 species of the bat family. Most of these are small animals which eat insects or fruit. Again, however, the range of animals within the family is enormous: from the large fruit bats or flying foxes that live in huge camps of up to 50 000, to the tiny Queensland blossom bats only five centimetres long.

Above left: Aboriginals probably brought dingoes to Australia as hunting dogs. Unlike domestic dogs their ears remain erect and they have an eerie howl instead of a bark.

Far left: A flying fox rests, hanging on a limb. These large bats were named because of their sharp, fox-like faces and furry bodies.

Above and left: Australian fur seals. These are the largest fur seals in the world, weighing up to 360 kilograms. Each male has a harem of up to 50 females. The mother suckles her pup until it is a month old and then feeds it spasmodically for another seven months.

Mammals of the Desert

The inhospitable land of central Australia is home for a variety of mammals. In addition to the well-known and easily discernible red kangaroos, euros (or hill kangaroos) and dingoes, there are a host of tiny native mammals, often unseen because of their nocturnal habits. Some, like the bilby, are marsupials; others, small as they are, are placental mammals. Among the best adapted of the desert mammals is the hopping mouse. With its long brush-tipped tail and large hind limbs, this tiny nocturnal rodent looks like a miniature kangaroo. It survives the heat of the interior by spending its days deep underground in a burrow that may drop vertically for more than a metre before turning sharply to become a horizontal tunnel. In a nest at the end, the babies are born, suckled and protected until they can fend for themselves.

Many of the small nocturnal desert animals are rarely seen and scientists are still extending their knowledge of the region's fauna.

Far left: A family of fat-tailed marsupial mice.

Below left: A tiny marsupial of the Ningaui family.

Left: A pouched mouse in the dunnart family.

Below centre: A kowari or Byrne's marsupial mouse.

Below: One of the nine species of hopping mice.

Perhaps a hundred million years ago there came to Australia reptiles that were already showing some mammal-like characteristics. Today these prehistoric animals have only two descendants: the echidna and the platypus. These living fossils share a curious combination of features, some akin to those of reptiles, others firmly belonging to the mammals. Because of their distinctive evolutionary niche, the platypus and echidna have a separate class within the mammal family: they are the only two *monotremes* in the world.

When the first platypus skins were sent to England, scientists believed they were victims of a practical joke. Here was an animal with a leathery bill like that of a duck, webbed feet and a flat, rudder-like tail. Its skin was covered with fur and, like other mammals, its young were suckled by milk from the mother's body. But its bones more closely resembled those of a reptile and, most amazing of all, it laid eggs. Platypuses live in streams and lakes throughout eastern Australia. Before laying her eggs a female platypus digs a burrow, up to 27 metres long, in the river bank. At the end she builds a nest of leaves and grass where she lays her two soft eggs. The tiny, 15-millimetre babies hatch within ten days but they stay in the nest, suckling milk, for another four months until they are 30 centimetres long.

With their sharp spines and long tube-like muzzles, echidnas look very different from their relatives the platypuses. The female lays one leathery egg and carries it in a pouch which only forms in the breeding season. The echidna's spines protect it well and, unlike most small mammals, it forages openly during the day, probing with its long sticky tongue for ants and termites.

Left and above left: Echidnas thrust their long tubular snouts under logs, bark and stones to probe for ants, grubs and termites. Then the long sticky tongue darts in and out gathering the food.

Above: The platypus relies on its sensitive leathery muzzle to search out food underwater.

Birds

Australians, like people everywhere, are fascinated by birds. From time immemorial earthbound humans have envied and tried to emulate the bird's ability to fly. Even in an age of supersonic aircraft and manned space flight we still gaze with wonder at the graceful flight of a bird. We also treasure birds for their beauty, both of colour and song, and many a poet has celebrated these qualities in verse.

It is, perhaps, a little ironic that Australia's best-known bird is flightless, is uniformly drab in colour and emits a kind of grunting sound that is anything but musical. The emu is Australia's largest bird and one of its fastest-moving animals. When chased it can race along at almost 50 kilometres an hour.

At the other end of the scale are the many varieties of tiny finches, robins, wrens and small honeyeaters. Many of these can be seen flitting about suburban gardens searching for insects or delving with delicately curved beaks into blossoms in quest of their nectar. One of the most attractive of these is the splendid blue wren, unmistakable with its erect tail and brilliant hues.

In between is a vast range of birds of all shapes, sizes and colours and displaying a rich variety of habitat and lifestyle. There are more than 700 known species of birds in Australia and more than half of them are unique to this country. Included in this array are water birds, parrots, wading birds, owls and other birds of prey as well as flycatchers and honeyeaters.

Many of them, like the emu, are spread widely throughout the country. Others live only or predominantly in environments to which they are specially suited. As a result, some of Australia's most interesting birds are rarely seen by urban

dwellers. The beautifully plumaged cassowary lives only in the lush rainforests of northern Queensland, while the famous dancing brolga is one of a number of long-legged wading birds which inhabit the swampy plains of northern Australia.

Among the most colourful of Australian birds are the many members of the parrot family which includes galahs, sulphur-crested cockatoos, rosellas, lorikeets and that most popular of caged birds, the budgerigar. This small parrot, in its wild state, is an inhabitant of the dry inland areas where it flies about in large flocks, bringing the desert to life with splashes of brilliant green and yellow.

Birds are an essential part of our country's natural environment. They are, too, part of our cultural heritage and figure largely in Aboriginal legends as well as in the literature and art of white Australians.

The Parrot Family

The birds of the parrot family are undoubtedly the most colourful and attractive in Australia. Ranging from the majestic crested palm cockatoos of northern Queensland, through the screeching coloured galahs, lorikeets, parrots and rosellas, to the tiny budgerigars that fly in flocks through the inland, the 55 members of the parrot family are widely distributed throughout the continent.

All the parrots have unusual feet, for two toes point backwards while the other two point forwards. This allows parrots to cling or grasp more easily and they can use one foot as a hand to hold food. All parrots, too, have distinctive hooked beaks. Lorikeets, unlike cockatoos and other parrots, have brush-like tongues for sucking nectar and pollen.

Three colourful members of the parrot family. Rainbow lorikeets (left) are easily tamed and are often fed in suburban gardens. The red-winged parrot (above left), on the other hand, is shy and takes to the air when approached. The beautifully marked eclectus parrot (above) was not discovered until 1913. It is found only in Cape York.

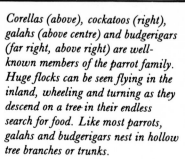

Corellas (above), cockatoos (right), galahs (above centre) and budgerigars (far right, above right) are well-known members of the parrot family. Huge flocks can be seen flying in the inland, wheeling and turning as they descend on a tree in their endless search for food. Like most parrots, galahs and budgerigars nest in hollow tree branches or trunks.

Owls

There are two families of owls in Australia. Rufous, powerful, boobook and barking owls belong to the Ninox family. By far the most common is the boobook or mopoke owl, named after its distinctive two-syllabled cry, which is found throughout the continent. Like other owls, the boobook eats smaller birds and mammals, especially mice which it catches with the help of its sensitive ears. The barking owl is sometimes named the 'screaming woman owl' because it occasionally produces a terrifying high-pitched scream instead of its usual barking sound. This owl is found in woodland and forests throughout much of Australia.

Barn owls, masked owls, sooty owls and grass owls all belong to the Tyto family. They are distinguishable by their heart-shaped facial discs which give them the somewhat startled eccentric faces that are usually associated with owls. Like so many other animals, these owls have adapted to their particular environment: masked owls in the Nullarbor roost in caves rather than trees, and grass owls have unusually long legs to make life easier in the grassy, often swampy tussocks they inhabit.

Far left: A masked owl. In parts of Australia these birds are encouraged because they prey on rabbits.

Centre left: Although it is found throughout Australia, the barn owl is rarely seen because of its nocturnal habits.

Above and left: The boobook owl is one of Australia's smallest. During the day it remains motionless, well camouflaged by its tawny feathers. At night the boobook comes to life and searches for the small birds, mice and insects that are its prey. This search is made easier by the owl's soundless flight, its sharp hearing, and by the sensitive feathers around its eyes which respond to noises. The boobook is sometimes called a mopoke owl, both names deriving from the bird's cry.

Birds of Prey

Every habitat in Australia supports one or more kinds of birds of prey. Sea eagles and ospreys can be seen hovering over much of the coastline, swamp harriers prefer the marshes, while many birds of prey such as the whistling kite, sparrowhawk, goshawk and nankeen kestrel are distributed throughout the continent.

There are three families of diurnal birds of prey in Australia in addition to the nocturnal owls. The biggest family, Accipitridae, contains the eagles, hawks, kites, goshawks and harriers. The largest Australian bird of prey is the mighty wedgetailed eagle whose wing span measures up to two and a half metres. In the past this magnificent bird was killed in thousands by farmers who feared its reputation as a killer of lambs. More recently their part in destroying rabbits has been appreciated.

The osprey is the only Australian representative of the Pandionidae family. Singly and in pairs these dark brown and white birds cruise the coastline in search of fish.

Finally there are the falcons, of which Australia has six types. Their speed, accuracy and deadly efficiency combine to make the falcons one of nature's masterpieces, superbly built for their task of attacking and killing their prey.

Three members of the Accipitridae family.

Far left and above left: Wedgetailed eagles, Australia's largest birds of prey.

Above top: A whistling kite whose penetrating whistle can be heard for a kilometre.

Above and right: White-breasted sea eagle.

Birds of River, Lake and Ocean

Most Australian water birds are coastal dwellers but there are some which thrive in the lakes, swamps and billabongs of the inland rivers. When the rivers flow after heavy rain, birds such as black swans, ducks, white-faced herons, pied stilts and darters descend and breed quickly while water is plentiful.

Many of our coastal birds are visitors escaping the harsh winter of the northern hemisphere. Others are temporary migrants from Asia or the islands near Antarctica. Most common are the waders, gulls and terns. The silver gull, or comon seagull, is the best known of all for it thrives not only along the coast but also well into the inland along the river systems. Terns, sometimes called sea-swallows, are smaller than the gulls but, like them, nest in large, noisy communities.

Pelicans, gannets, darters and cormorants are related. All have elongated sharp beaks for catching fish. Unlike other water birds, however, cormorants and darters do not have waterproof feathers. After swimming and diving they must rest on land with their wings outstretched to dry off.

Far left and centre left: Sooty terns are common along the northern coast. They breed in noisy colonies. Adults may spend several months in distant lands and then return to the very colony where they were hatched.

Left and below left: Although recognised as the emblem of Western Australia, black swans are widely distributed across southern Australia. They moult between September and February. At this time they are flightless and gather in large flocks on lakes and rivers.

Below: A heron in silhouette.

Six distinctive water birds.

Far left: A flock of whistling ducks. These darkly plumaged birds are found along the northern coast.

Below left: Two kinds of cormorants. The little black cormorant (far left) grows 61 centimetres tall and is common in inland waters while the pied cormorant (centre left) grows to 76 centimetres and usually lives along the coast.

Left: Gannets nesting near the Great Barrier Reef.

Below centre: The darter, sometimes called the snake bird.

Below: Pelicans have lived in Australia for over 30 million years.

Perching Birds

By far the largest group of birds in Australia are the 34 families of perching birds, often called passerines or songbirds. The distinctive formation of their toes helps them to cling safely to branches while their voiceboxes are more specialised than those of other birds, enabling them to sing, often very beautifully.

Among the hundreds of passerines are the pittas, lyrebirds, larks, wagtails, thrushes, babblers, wrens, honeyeaters, chats, currawongs and silvereyes. While many of them are plain little birds, others like the tiny zebra finch, the chats and wrens are beautifully coloured and distinctively marked. Some, like the lyrebirds and bower birds, are notable for their unique behaviour patterns.

Below left: A white-winged triller feeds its hungry nestlings. Both males and females share the tasks of building a nest, incubating and rearing the chicks.

Left: Zebra finches, the smallest and most common Australian finches, are named because of their black and white striped tails.

Below centre: The butcherbird is aptly named for it kills and eats young birds as well as mice, insects and lizards.

Below: A male splendid blue wren. The female is much duller, with greyish brown feathers and a brown eye patch.

Feeding the young is an important task for bird parents, just as it is for other animals.

Above left: A willie wagtail attends to its nestlings. The neat, cup-shaped nest is usually built in a tree fork and is made from fine grass bound with cobwebs. Both parents help to feed the young.

Far left: With their mouths open, baby thrushes await the return of their parents.

Centre left: A male flame robin at its nest. With its dark grey back and brilliant orange-red front this robin is a distinctive sight in the grassy areas of southeast Australia which are its habitat.

Above: A spotted or western bower bird stands outside its bower, built from two parallel walls of carefully woven sticks.

Left: A lyrebird performs its distinctive courting dance. Its splendid tail is outstretched and brought forward like an open fan.

Reptiles

Australia has more than its fair share of reptiles: 300 species of lizards, 140 species of snakes, two kinds of crocodiles and several types of turtles and tortoises. Many of these animals have relatives in Asia and South America; some, however, like the legless lizards, are unique to Australia.

All reptiles have a scaly skin and those with legs usually seem to be squatting because of the way their legs join the body. Unlike mammals, reptiles cannot easily control their body temperature. During the day they bask in the sun to keep warm, but if it becomes too hot they shelter under logs or behind stones.

Some skinks in the lizard family grow only five centimetres long while the saltwater crocodile reaches six metres. But size becomes irrelevant when a reptile has to defend itself. It is as difficult to see a giant crocodile in muddy water as a tiny skink in the desert sand. Some harmless lizards have fearsome looking frills or beards to frighten predators; others can shed part of their body when captured.

The saltwater crocodile and about 20 kinds of Australian snakes are dangerous, even fatal, to humans but, despite their sometimes fierce appearance, most of the reptiles of Australia are harmless.

Crocodiles and Tortoises

Two species of crocodiles are found in Australia. Small harmless freshwater crocodiles can be seen in inland rivers and swamps, while the larger, more powerful saltwater crocodiles live in estuaries. The main difference between the two species lies in the shape of the snout.

Tortoises belong to an ancient order of reptiles, relatively unchanged for 200 million years. Australian native tortoises are freshwater animals with legs and webbed feet. Marine turtles have swimming flippers.

The saltwater crocodile (centre left and above) usually grows between five and seven metres long and will attack humans, horses and cattle. In the past these huge reptiles have been heavily slaughtered for their skins.

Far left: A freshwater crocodile lies well disguised in muddy water. This crocodile, which grows to three metres, is harmless to humans and feeds on fish and other water life.

Centre right: The massive head of a loggerhead turtle.

43

Australia's snakes are found throughout the continent and their appearance, structure and behaviour are adapted to a variety of distinctive habitats.

The copperhead (above top), death adder (above), taipan (middle centre), brown snake (above far right) and carpet snake (far right) are land dwellers, although some of them spend part of their time in water or trees. The tiger snake (above centre) inhabits swampy areas while the olive sea snake (above right) moves through the water like an eel and the green tree snake (right) is arboreal.

44

Snakes

Australian snakes are numerous and varied. They range from tiny blind snakes that feed on ants and termites to the large, sleek and deadly taipan. There are snakes whose eyes and nostrils can be blocked to enable them to swim underwater. Most of these sea snakes need never come on land for their live young are born in the water. Other snakes are tree dwellers, although the most common, the green tree snake, is also a good swimmer and likes to bask on the ground around caves and rocks.

There are about 130 species of snakes in Australia, grouped into five families. The largest family, with 70 kinds of snakes, is the elapid group. Although all the snakes in this family are venomous, most are small and harmless to humans.

Lizards

Australian lizards form five distinct family groups. Most common are the skinks. There are over 150 kinds of these smooth-scaled, slender lizards, most of which are quite small. One of the largest skinks is the well-known blue-tongue lizard, with its stout body and darting blue tongue.

Geckoes are another large group of lizards. Unlike the skinks they are nocturnal. Among this family is the knob-tailed gecko (above) which inhabits inland Australia.

Then there are the dragons, an aptly named group of lizards with blunt heads, rough skin and thick legs. Dragons have a varied collection of beards, crests, frills and spikes with which to frighten their enemies. The Boyd's forest dragon (right) lives deep in Queensland's rainforests.

Goannas or monitor lizards (above top) are common in most parts of Australia for they have adapted to a wide range of habitats. Many are tree-climbers while others spend most of their time in water.

Unique to Australia are the legless or snake lizards which have lost their limbs. Unlike snakes, however, they have visible ears and many have scaly flaps as a reminder of where their hind limbs once were.

Far left: A frilled lizard. When the lizard is disturbed it opens its mouth and hisses fiercely. It also raises the frill or ruff like an umbrella.

Left: A shingleback or stumpy-tailed lizard. This bulky lizard protects itself by hissing and poking out its tongue.

Below centre: The head of a perentie, the second largest lizard in the world.

Below: A thorny devil. This grotesque lizard is covered with sharp spikes.

Amphibians

There are 2500 species of frogs and toads throughout the world but only 150 of them are found in Australia. There are no native Australian toads but one species, *Bufo marinus* or cane toad, was brought to Queensland in 1935 to control the cane beetle that was damaging sugar crops. This hardy, warty amphibian has thrived and extended its habitat and its poison glands have caused the deaths of many snakes, birds, cats and dogs.

More attractive and much less harmful are the 20 kinds of tree frogs found in northern New South Wales and Queensland. Their supple limbs and thick suction pads enable these insect-eating amphibians to cling tenaciously to tree branches while resting during the day.

One of the most unusual Australian frogs is the water-holding frog which frequents the arid desert regions. It can store large amounts of water in its bladder, which swells up like a balloon. During drought the frog burrows deep into the ground where it survives for several years if necessary until the next rains come.

Above left: The green and golden bell frog is common in eastern New South Wales.

Above top: A green tree frog.

Left: Bufo marinus, *the introduced cane toad.*

Above: A trilling frog, widespread across the centre of the continent.

Insects and Spiders

Four of Australia's 40 000 kinds of insects.

Above top: This stick insect is well camouflaged in a tree branch.

Above: A file of caterpillars makes its way across the desert.

Right: A mantid feasting on a cicada.

Far right: A dragonfly, looking rather like a helicopter about to take off.

At least 55 000 kinds of insects are known in Australia and there may, in fact, be double that number for many kinds of insects are rarely seen, because they are so tiny and they spend their lives in remote spots.

Adult insects have three pairs of legs and their bodies are divided into three distinct parts — the head, thorax and abdomen. Insects have a pair of antennae or feelers and many, but not all, have one or two pairs of wings. In these respects insects are distinguished from other forms of life. But beyond these common features insects have developed a variety of amazing shapes, colours and habits.

Insects live on the ground, under the ground and above the ground. They live in water, on trees or in the bodies of other living creatures. Some, like the ants, have developed complex communities and elaborate divisions of labour. Many — perhaps 600 — are pests whose control and management cost millions of dollars each year. Others contribute significantly to a sound ecological balance while many are admired for their beauty and colour.

About 1700 of the world's 40 000 kinds of spiders are found in Australia. They range in size from tiny, almost imperceptible creatures to animals large enough to kill and eat a bird. Their habitats, too, vary enormously. Spiders live in caves, along the seashore, in the desert, under rocks, in snow country, under the ground and in gardens.

Very few Australian spiders are dangerous to humans although several can give a painful sting. The widest-spread poisonous spider is the red-back but the most lethal is the funnel-web, a large, black, heavily-built spider with venomous fangs.

There are over 250 species of butterflies in Australia. Among them are the blue triangle (above top), wanderer (above) and spotted skipper (above right).

Right: A cicada. When cicada eggs hatch the larvae burrow underground where they spend one or more years feeding on sap. The fully grown cicada emerges as a winged adult.

Most of Australia's insects are beetles for there are at least 20 000 species throughout the continent. All beetles have six legs and hard wing cases, and most have a pair of antennae and biting jaws. As these species show, the wing cases of beetles can be beautifully patterned.

Right: The brilliantly marked diamond weevil has a bright metallic shine.

Below: Beetles of the Christmas or king beetle family.

Among the most common Australian spiders are the orb-weavers of the Argiopidae family. At dusk they build large snares between two objects to trap night-flying insects. During the day the spider remains hidden nearby.

Above: The beautifully delicate web of an orb-building spider.

Left: A garden orb-weaver, sometimes called a cart-wheel spider. These spiders occur widely over Australia but their colour and patterns vary considerably.

Fish

The fish in Australian waters come in an incredible variety of sizes, colours and shapes. Some live in constant darkness in the deep water beyond the continental shelf. Others stay close to the coral of the Great Barrier Reef. There are more than 130 native freshwater fish, the largest of which is the Murray cod which can weigh up to 90 kilograms. The most ancient of these freshwater species is the Queensland lungfish which dates back almost 400 million years.

The most numerous and undoubtedly the most beautiful of Australia's fish are those which live in tropical waters. Coral or butterfly fish and their relatives, the angel fish, are the most brightly coloured. Their jaws are specially adapted to allow them to pick from the coral reefs the tiny invertebrates and polyps that make up their food. Then there are the cleaner fish which, in return for protection, will clean other fish of parasites, even going into the larger fish's mouth and gills to ensure a thorough job.

Some of these fish of the tropics are dangerous to humans. Many, like the scorpion fish and butterfly cod, have sharp spines which can inflict painful stings. Others, such as the porcupine fish and pufferfish, have poisonous flesh.

Right: Anemone fish live among the tentacles of sea anemones. They are immune to the stinging cells that poison other small fish.

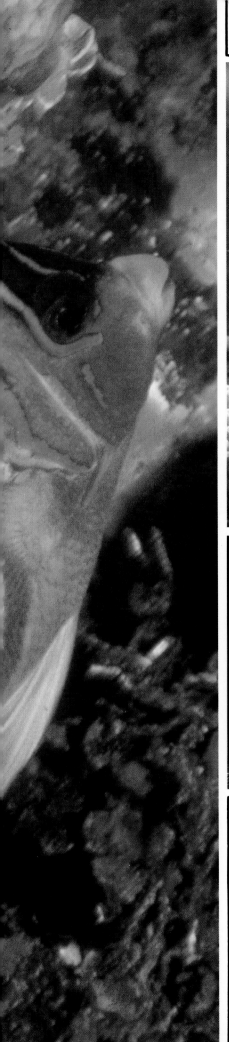

The coral reefs off the coast of Queensland shelter hundreds of kinds of colourful fish.

Left: The royal angelfish, or blue band angel, grows to 30 centimetres long.

Above top: The well-camouflaged butterfly cod can inflict a painful sting if handled.

Above: A beautifully coloured threadfin coral fish.